Animal Blues

Ben,
Keep the faith
and keep the animals
safe!
[illegible]

by James Clarke-Coley

First Published: November 2024
by
Budding Authors Assistant
www.help2publish.co.uk

ISBN: 9781917128056

INTRODUCTION

The inspiration behind Animal Blues was primarily the plight of nature around the globe. It is not a 'doomsday warning' although many of my poems may reflect this viewpoint – it's just a cry from the soul. There are many wonderful people, who are indeed taking serious action to save animals from extinction. The poems include some self-deprecating humour, hopefully all is not doom and gloom.

My Grandsons were a major reason for my poetry. To let them know I wanted to preserve the beauty of animals for them.

I have lent the rhythm of the American soul and rap singers and the protest singers of the 60's such as Bob Dylan, Marvin Gaye, Joni Mitchell. The poet pop/rock stars like Leonard Cohen and Bruce Springsteen have a similar motivating influence. However, the key driver is the animals themselves, their unique traits, beauty and wonderous talents that we often miss.

I hope you enjoy the collection and if they touch you as the animals have touched me, it will be very much 'like the blues'.

DEDICATION

To my loving wife, Tricia, for her support and patience, remembering artists are always poor...

CONTENTS

Thank you for supporting The RUR River Charity

An Epitaph to a Pine Marten

Appearing from the popping gorse,
Camouflaged by day of course.
Flash of beauty till now unseen,
He's never where he should have been.

All stealth in sound and light of step,
Ears pricked, darting, lithe, adept.
His in-built caution we all can see,
Even a dozy 'townee' like me.

Finally settled, but never secure,
From hungry talon, bullet, or claw.
Nothing for him was quiet or still,
Ever wary of those that kill.

Each sound and stir seemed to say,
Be careful, on guard, do not stay.
His fox-like ears and pointed nose,
And yellow bib and dainty toes.

Creature of beauty and yet so rare.
Why so scarce it isn't fair?
For stealing eggs, hunted, slain,
Caught in traps, died in pain.

He looked at me as if to say,
What further price must I pay?
I wasn't silver, neither gold,
Nor a secret never to be told.

No rhyme, no epitaph for me,
I can't even die in dignity.
You're the reason and your kind,
That I'm so very hard to find.

The dying world has become devoid,
Of the creatures you have destroyed.
A paradise on Earth was lost.
Destroying beauty - but at what cost?

City Dweller

‘Reynard, Reynard you’ve lost your soul,
Your urban life has taken its toll.
You beg and steal from this human space.
From the very people who killed your race’.

‘But Country Cousin, see my coat,
Smooth as ermine just like a stoat.
Eyes that shine all bright and clear,
I’m far better off living here.

Look at you, you’ll never change,
Dirty, bony and full of mange.
Rabbit with mixy or a mouse,
Caught you chomping on a louse’.

‘Thing is Reynard you’ve lost the plot.
Yes, the Vixens think you’re hot,
But I live free under the stars,
A life of Riley; apart from the cars.

The country air, fresh and clean,
Like a knife so sharp and keen.
I sniff ripening rape and sage,
Not like the smells in your deluded cage’.

'No burgers for me, no scraps from tins,
Y'see, I don't have to eat out of bins.
Why can't you see the invisible trap,
Do I have to sit and draw you a map?

For comfort, you've given up on you,
Just like all your blind humans too.
Then what of you cousin dear,
When new friends are no longer here'.

Hare Raising

March is here, cherry is showing,
Farmers finally finished sowing.
Safe from lampers' lurchers run,
Long shanks Hare now having fun.
Leant against the old wire fence,
Looking more than a little tense.

Built lean and lithe as a cat,
Limbs long, trained, no fat.
The boxers' eyes narrowed as they met,
'Sugar Ray' and contender set.

The champion ducked and dived by habit.
His corner man said, 'He's a rabbit',
'Flaming big rabbit' says a dubious Ray,
'Keep your dukes up, he'll never stay'.

'He may be big, he may be tall,
The bigger they are, the harder they fall!'
'Thanks for your pearls of wisdom,
But I ain't in this just for fun'.

The champion's eyes stared and sent,
A message filled with rare intent.
Springing off the fence to dance,
You'll need more than that to stand a chance,

Said contender 'Tyson' to his foe,
'I'll just leap over and stand on your toe!'

Ray started to shadow box and tease,
The watching girls went weak at the knees.
They circled each other, light on their toes,
Squeals of delight from the watching Does.

In a flash they rose full height,
Readying for the coming fight.
Paws a blur as they met,
Hesitation but not finished yet.

Once more, with fighters looking hurt,
But suddenly Tyson hit the dirt.
His limp form was whisked away,
The champion will fight another day.

Another Otter Hunt

Sleek, smooth, shining, slipping below,
Luminous trail of bubbles as they go.
With a shake of the head, a flick of the ear,
As they were gone, would re-appear.

Muzzles silver, whiskers glistening,
Playful duet but always listening.
Onto their backs, they clutch a crab,
Saturday drunk with a lamb Kebab.

They wolf it down, always sharing,
With their pups, so very caring.
Mum's milk for the lazy brood,
Spending their time catching food.

Sleek thick fur, slick polished oil,
A racing turn made the water boil.
The molluscs, anxious; panic below,
Caught up; a swirling undertow.

Oh feast, feast while you can,
Fast approaching there comes a man.
He's not the prospect of menacing threat,
Just his four-legged murderous pet.

The pair evaporate away,
Leaving no trace of where they play.
To protect, to nurture is their creed,
Saving their pups from the canine greed.

Emperor of the Skies – or Was It?

A keening cry broke the still,
Clean Scottish air by the hill.
Excited, thrilled, pointing looking,
'It's got fingers' said Sarah hoping.

Our own Hamza was in a mess,
Camera stuck in a new harness.
The bird swooped and soared,
Our own aerial show never bored.

Oh, hold on what was that?
Looks like our hero was having a spat.
Being swallow dived by cocky crows,
But careful not to get too close.

He circled and hovered above to spot,
Now the camera was clicking, red hot.
'It's a Goldie' said Sarah with glee,
'If it is, that's four to me!'

No conclusion could be drawn,
Argued as we did till dawn,
Malt flowed, we checked the map,
A Golden Eagle, not on this App.
'Don't care', squiffy Sarah replied,
'See another, that's me on five!'

Two by Two

The clouds boiling, the sky slate black,
There was so much more to pack.
Now see Noah, checking the tide,
Heard a ruckus from outside.

Ezra appeared 'we need to talk,
You said 2 of a kind, would make the walk.
Well, I've got 3 Zebras and 1 horse,
The problem's the spare zebra of course.
He says he is identifying different today,
He'd like us to see his stripes, OK?'

With brewing skies and still no rain,
Noah wanted more haste, less pain.
Problems to solve, he was no saint,
He went downstairs to find some paint.

He spoke to Ezra to calm the rush,
Sent him outside with a brush.
With a carefully managed stroke,
He made the 'zebra' completely woke.

The paint will wash off in rain,
He'll transform into a horse again.
'Now Ezra, check the oats and grain,
We won't be touching land again'.

'Boss, the Tigers won't be feeding here,
They've just seen the Fallow deer.'
'Didn't they get the note' he sighed,
'Tigers were spammed,' Ezra cried.
'Well, they'll have to do their best,
Becoming Vegan like all the rest!

An Owl Without a Barn

A shimmering gleam of rust and white,
Swoops then hovers like a kite.
Quartering the field eyes never fail,
To catch a rodent urine trail.

So silent, his feathers light of weight,
Mean his prey hear far too late.
Mouse or vole in talons of steel,
Back to his chicks, another meal.

On one fateful day in May,
A road was built, in his way.
The opening traffic, in morning light,
Would increase ten-fold by that night.

As he flew searching for quarry,
Unaware, of the high-sided lorry.
It cut across his intended path,
An explosion of blood, the aftermath.

Evening came, no dad appears,
Mum couldn't dry their tiny tears.
No more food for the nest,
Another cruel statistic with the rest.

Prince Charming

Prince of the Glen, without a care,
Ten-point antler of regal air.
Prancing stag, not known to fall,
Light-stepping courtier at a Royal Ball.

Ruling over your vast domain,
Mountains, hill, field or lane.
Suede antlers, now crown of bone,
High-country weathered muscle tone.

Looking, turn, searching aware,
Hikers sudden trudging scare.
As you appear, in any weather,
Dancing run in purpling heather.

Velvet dusk, seek lower ground,
Often looked for, rarely found.
Huge ears, like a radar sensing,
Your kingdom with redundant fencing.

Ruling all you can survey,
Alpha Wolf is kept at bay.
With your top predator in retreat,
The danger is man's lust for meat.

Wary of them small or large,
Wearing green, brown camouflage.
They will hunt you down, or pretend,
It's in the name of farm and tend.

They'll trap and shoot, your blood they spill,
They call it cull, those who kill.
But it's life's balance they upset,
We must live with that regret.

Cold Hart

Soft rain painting each green brighter
Purpling heather carpet glisten
Stillness broken, who will listen
Hooves would thunder but whisper lighter

Steam rises from the sweating deer
Terror from those baying hounds
Seeking safer higher grounds
Child inside; she must break clear

Not there yet; The woods draw near
Whisper sound, whoosh of air
Slow motion, crumples in despair
As if strings cut by a puppeteer

Men stand smoking by soulless meat
Different shots in approaching dawn
Cruellest selfie with mother and fawn
Poachers throw the hounds a treat

Gang spies fast encroaching light
Shouldering rifles, lens cap on
Poacher's telescopic weapon
Greed is the shot, but man is the sight

Quietly loading lifeless carcass
Mother and child with no name
Their spirits flown such a shame
Soft wind sought their last caress

Summer is Here!

They herald summer, hear them fly,
The droning buzz, not very high.
Drawn to the pollen, attach to sow,
Fix to unsuspecting legs below.

Is there a better sound, so cosy,
Warming bumble bee, still dozy?
Pungent scent wafts below,
From flower to flower they're sure to go.

Purpling blossoms receive a guest,
Blooms opening at their behest.
Sweet nectar offered to a friend,
In homage to the wind, they bend.

Honeybee girls, working for queen,
Manuka and wax, busy, unseen.
Drones, no use, no sting,
Lazy, good for just one thing.

What use man's technology,
Without them no ecology.
Bees working in their hive,
Help the natural world survive.

Now be careful, here's the thing,
Don't just see them for their sting.
Remove those thoughts from your head,
Without the bees we won't be fed.

THIEF IN THE NIGHT

With his mask of black and white,
Bill, the burglar is out tonight.
He'll rob your nest of young,
Pinch ripening fruit still hung.

Badger eats all to the core,
This naughty, thieving omnivore.
They fight with fury, so able,
No stealing from his food table.

His strength of bite and power,
Make even hedgehogs hide and cower.
For Mr Brock fears no prickle,
If he's hungry, it will only tickle.

The thing that makes him afraid,
Is a man with dog and spade.
Who is able with impunity,
To kill the suspect carrier of TB.
To protect the cattle who,
Probably gave them the TB too.

KILLER FASHION ICON

Seeming harmless in babbling stream,
Belies a Mink killing mean.
Our migrant gift from the yanks,
Found a place on our riverbanks.

Within a decade, not long,
Ratty, the water vole had gone.
Then they turned their savage scowl,
On the local fish and fowl.

Enter our heroes, as needs must,
Norfolk and Suffolk River Trust.
Using a floating raft trap, so sure,
Removed the Mink from Yare to Bure.
Now they are moving towards the West,
To eradicate the invasive pest.

What price a fashion coat of fur?
Animal Libbers caused a stir?
Set free a killer, that was that,
Destroyed our native habitat.
Released a parasite they sought,
Into our rivers, without a thought.

Four for a Boy

Magpie, black and white, no poise,
Teen out on a night with the boys.
But majestic in air, swooping low,
Diving, chattering warning foe.

The child finds a poor chick,
All feathered but very sick.
Cupped in his gentle grip,
To Mum, careful of any slip.

'Can't keep him they steal!'
Followed entreaty and boyish appeal,
'But he's hurt, Mum, he fell',
Can I keep him, until he's well?'
Deaf to the answer in his head,
Kept in a box by the bed.

A few weeks later, wing on the mend,
The boy, to dad, mum did send.
'Now, son', father said, strangely mild,
'He's not a toy, he needs the wild.

He'll fly one day and then be lost,
Let him go don't count the cost.'
Tears, fought back, still show,
'He won't leave me now, I know.'

Holidays over back to school,
Kicking a ball and playing the fool.
Biking to school, the hill at a run,
Feet off the pedals, hair back. What fun.
People watched like a scene from Mars,
A Magpie on his handlebars.

The bird would wait, sitting alone,
Waiting for a lift back home.
What a thrill for the boy,
Touching the wild, what joy.
Is it true about the lad?
Certainly is, it was my dad!

There's a Murder

There's a murder, claimed the D.I.
Not us, grassed the magpie.
It's not a death, just some crows,
A theft of gems and on their toes.

Must be those crows for sure,
Intellectual as an overture.
Heads-up takes on any task,
Seeing through what you ask.

They're OK, just a little craven,
Said the jackdaw and the raven.
'Smart as whips, certainly sly,'
Said the rooks on the fly.

'It's not us, it's a mag-lie,
Framed by those thieving magpie.
We've been fitted up, crows confess,
Search our gaff, no body, no mess'.

We don't launder, or do coke,
As for murder that's a joke.
A bit of petty theft,
Of any BBQ that's left'.

We're all in gangs, see the signs,
Even crossing 'County-lines'.
Don't go near our hidden nest,
Keep clear, just for the best.

Search that vacant chimney,
Spy the stolen jewellery.
Certainly, made those ladies weep,
Unless you're a lucky chimney sweep!

The Birds Stopped Singing

The fog swirled in the acrid air,
Melancholic bells faded, take care.
Girls happy in the day, now scared,
How much better if someone cared.

Feathered flocking the square mile,
They perch shivering, forced to smile.
Scarlet, white face, gilded gold,
A different colour in the cold.
Many warnings not to go,
Street corner singing just for show.

Borne out of Victorian times,
Evil hunting on last chimes.
Moving stealthy, prey to catch,
Traps to set, plots to hatch.

Quietening air, the songs grew still,
'Cat the Ripper' moved to kill.
Thirty million songbirds a year,
Their sweet song we'll never hear.

After killing, cat starts to play,
When dead, sniffs, and slinks away.
The bird died badly, and in vain,
The Ripper loves the ghastly pain.

He fulfils some Psycatic thrill,
Like human twin, born to kill.

Wouldn't want to generalise,
To accuse all cats isn't wise.
There are many, gentle; Kept,
Domesticated, much-loved pet.
Fair of face and to boot,
See a mouse, won't give a hoot.

Forever been a worshipped kind,
Pharaohs and witches spring to mind.
When curled upon the lap, it seems,
We'll never know those feline dreams.

You Can Take a Baboon to Water

Under the searing sun, he stands,
Rheumy eyes, scanning his lands.
Short, tough as teak, light as lace,
Grizzled hair, life etched his face.
He is the leader of his tribe,
Needing water, to survive.

Look for primate, but not to kill,
Search for water, use his skill.
Need wily tracker take the lead,
The crafty trap must succeed.

Baboon troop, curious and bold,
A hollow tree, with fruit to hold.
The Boss makes a grab, that's the law,
The hole is too small, for fruit and paw.
He can't withdraw he's trapped, indeed,
Not by binding, but by greed.

They feed him salt, dry as a bone,
Free him, track him, stay in zone.
He heads for the hidden water hollow,
Bushmen stooping, quietly follow.

Digging where the baboon shows,
Through the sand – yes! - the water flows.

With their buckskin bottles ready,
Fill them up, laughing, heady.
To survive this Kalahari heat,
Bushman thinking can't be beat.

The New Harpoon

Oh, beautiful behemoth sounding deep
travelling the seas while others sleep
swimming south with calf and cow
safe from Whalers, Green Peace vow.

Going to feed in colder climes
thriving in improving times
humpbacks, blues, minkes too
playing happy families, deep and true
no harpoons to dodge at sea
now facing a different enemy.

What of their turbulent palace
is it again a poison chalice?
From man's greed, so heretic
discarded, invisible, fatal plastic
it clogs the lungs, flows in blood
kills more painfully, than harpoons could.

Grey Bush Tucker

Oh dark invader from the West,
Gave our local Reds no rest.
So, they retreated North, far flung,
To find new forests for their young.

Who in their right mind,
Introduced a foreign kind?
When we had a russet beauty,
Perhaps he thought it was his duty.

Victorian Duke introduced the grey,
Did he know our reds would pay?
Carried disease, bully to measure,
To eradicate our native treasure.

The grey plague must be clear,
Before red squirrels re-appear.
Thank goodness Reds do still reign,
In Scottish woodlands, their domain.
Pine Marten will come again,
Reds can share the woods again.

We watch them twinkle, then bewitch,
Tufts on their ears, a sudden twitch.
Are they fairies from some lost fable?
Nibbling nuts on garden table.
As if with wings, they take flight,
A flash of orange, white so bright.
His U.S. cousin with a squark,
Cannon fodder for the hawk.

A Kite – New Flight?

Grace, greys, silvers, russet-browns,
The Kite sets sail above the Downs.
Mastering wind both high and low,
A thermal shift, red bird in tow.
Wing tip fingers finesse the breeze,
A pianist caressing ivory keys.

Chevron wings, will not impede,
The shift in gear at any speed.
Forked tail used as a rudder,
Movement sublime with little shudder.

In challenging winds, even a gale,
Her feathers always set the sail.
A mewling cry, is heard by all,
Her arrival delivered by clarion call.

The Kite was disappearing fast,
Who weighted that die to cast?
To save the grouse-shoots for the few,
Were they hunted and killed for you?

Some brave humans took a stance,
Preserve, protect our wildlife balance.
There were survivors in the south,
Beat the cull by word of mouth.

They wanted the red bird to live,
Having so much more to give.
They clear the carrion, which if left,
Spread disease, other lives bereft.

On the M40 'Zoo', they surely thrive,
Clearing roadkill to survive.
Badger, Hedgehog, fox and deer,
What's wrong with drivers, can't they steer?
The red kite back from the edge,
But others cower in the hedge.
Take with two hands, one to give,
Must we kill so they can live?

King of the Tundra

Blue moon making the world glow silver,
A voice so lonely, it could make you shiver.
The air feels cold and oh, so sharp,
More of a howl and less of a bark.
He's calling a mate in anticipation,
Meeting up will save his nation.

Worldly intellect, centuries old,
Tales to tell, blood runs cold.
Menace in those yellowing eyes,
Barrel chest, long sinewy thighs.
He's studied prey since time began,
No escape, they'll be out-ran.

The Alpha needs his pack to grow,
His wolf numbers extinction low.
With winter hard and food so scarce,
His extended family are less and less.
Killed by Cattlemen but not for food,
Used wicked poison and traps so crude.

The Alpha remembers when,
The hunters were the Spirit Men.
Mutual respect was their stance,
Similar music different dance.
On rare days they would meet,
There was nobility in defeat.
A wolf would die, the Sioux would sing,
Take a present for their King.

They'd skin a hide, take a fang,
Round their necks the tooth would hang.

Once proud predator, top of the chain,
He'll never be number one again.
Don't be fooled by the status loss,
Before you allow your paths to cross.
If you venture into the wild,
To him, you are just a child.
You can't see him today,
He sensed you so far away.
His howl scares both fowl and game,
If you were wise, you'd feel the same.
In a hunt they find their mark,
The slowest creature in the dark.
In the wild; no, not the caribou,
The slowest, dumbest beast is YOU!

Lady of the Loch

Regal Regent of Scottish Loch,
Lord Osprey flies taking stock.
Needs the fish for his chicks,
The laser eyes make their pick.
From failure he must refrain,
Or Lady sends him out again.

Wings flatten by evolved design,
A perfect Raptor, body and mind.
Underwater, prey take fright,
Transparent eyelids ensure his sight.
Exquisite Nature had a plan,
Contact Lens, before dawn of man.

Talons Zygodactyl to attack,
Claws to the front and to back.
He uses them to lock the trout,
Struggle, twist; There's no way out.
Back to the nest, fish to drop,
Before the chicks throw a strop.

His Lady sends him out again,
To forage food on her domain.
Was that a flicker in her eye,
As he circled once more to fly?
Was it a lest played chord?
'Not bad. Well-done Lord'.
Once more a blur of missile grey,

Into the Loch, all that day.
Nature's palette, perfect hue,
Painted silver scattered blue.

Only then seek gratitude,
Asked to share the family food.
Who has seen, the swoop the glide?
Only the watchers in the hide.

Once fledged, the chicks must fend,
Trained to hunt, skills to lend.
The parents must homeward fly,
To Africa's far-away limitless sky.
Five thousand miles with little rest,
In the Spring they return to nest.

A million years, evolved perfection,
Recent driven to extinction.
Shot for sport for those on high,
Hunted. How many ways to die?

Don't even have a chance to grow,
Eggs are stolen to put on show.
Legislation, and protection,
Saved the bird from destruction.

Scotland's lochs hold no fear,
Lady returns year after year.
She raised her chicks on platform high,
Her mate, once again, Prince of the sky.

A Moonlit Dinner for One

Glistening trail over autumn dew,
Luminescent to the moonlit view.
Lily strewn pond was quivering,
Blown bent teasel shivering.
Ripples, inhabitants unseen,
What do those bubbles mean?
Perhaps, Koi grubs for a meal,
Mysteries, darker dusk reveal.

A slug made its painful path,
Compost scrummage aftermath.
A closer study of the trail,
Arrow straight for Grandpa's kale.
Tomorrow they would count the cost,
Was it slugs or evening frost?

But this night – a different ending,
A message his trail was sending.
The air stood still and crisper,
Hardly a sound, more a whisper.
A head appears, eyes set back,
Living Queen, green and black.
A tongue flicks testing the air,
Only a radar could compare.
Testing the chemicals of her prey,
Her après had passed this way.

Green glassy, lithe and long,
Forever flicking out her tongue.
Grassy serpent, silent night,
Dry and smooth, harmless bite.
Unless a slug, frog or toad,
Should foolishly, cross her road.
Made a menu in her head,
Slug for starter. Frog parfait,
Washed down with worm sorbet.

Grandpa's kale was saved that night,
The slug didn't put up a fight,
Regal grass snake; Queen of the night.
A human garden is her site,
Surely a living testimony,
Of man and nature in harmony.

SPIRIT IN THE SKY

Peer in an eagle's tawny eye,
Discover then, why man must fly.
Wild, untamed, fierce and free,
Not content to roost a tree.

Soaring above the mountain snow,
Tells you all you need to know.
The fingered wings, two men across,
Wind, storm or gale would boss.

The eviscerating beak, talons of steel,
Prey soon spotted becomes a meal.
A bird filled with such savage rage,
Yet, so gentle with the young it raised.
A killing machine, born to fight,
No A.I. could design that flight.

Cherokee boy climbed eerie high,
With a fearful eye on the sky.
Mother would strike. Screeching love,
If danger to chicks was seen from above.

The boy would steal a feather with care,
Would wear it proudly in braided hair.
Triumphant return covered in blood,
His rite of passage to manhood.

Why recluse, and hard to find,
Aloof and distant from any kind?
From the mountain you came forth,
Did the cruel poachers drive you North?
Or was it a Prince upon a horse,
That needed you to hunt and course?

A Tern for the Worse

Sun beats down, air stagnant still,
Run into water, or never will.
Wearing hats or they'll be sick,
Ship Ahoy! Or Kiss me Quick.

Boys on slots, Kaleidoscope noise,
Walk the parade, shops with toys.
Girls buying candy, bubbles and books,
Naughty postcards, sneaky looks.

Quieted children hear Dingley-Dong,
It draws them in; That seaside song.
Girls giggling, boys with a tan,
Run to the singing, ice-cream van.

Breathless, standing two by two,
Jostling, eager in the queue.
A raspberry cone or ninety-nine,
Choices argued in the line.

Rosy-cheeked cherub holds her prize,
Just one lick and then; Surprise!
Bounty plucked she gave a cry,
Black-headed hoodlum of the sky.

The Gulls were circling, calling clear,
Swooping, diving, showed no fear.
Their ululating call filled the air,
Stealing food, where they dare.

Hooded, Common or Herring gull,
Join the flocks, the air is full.
Black faced tern and Kittiwakes,
Snatch the chips and ginger cakes.

Far from the beach on clifftop edge,
Nesting somewhere on the ledge.
Huge flocks await the summers wane,
Flying north to breed again.

Human habitat draws the few,
Refuse tips, playing fields too.
Amazing what we throw away,
Keeps a gull in food all day.

Buffalo Shame

A shimmering sun sets plains alight,
Dead Buffalo, a carnage scene below,
From eagle high a nightmare sight.
A massacre, with gun, not bow.

Bloodied pebbles on a beach shore,
Skinned for their hides, for fashion,
As far as the eye can see, and more.
Killed by men devoid of passion.

A prone man in furs, wets his fingers,
Remington rifle, mighty bore,
Massages the sight, sees what lingers.
Yes, a herd to kill, then a thousand more.

Dwindling herds, now hard to find,
Discarded hides, diminishing themes.
Extinction legacy left behind,
Now Bison only roam in dreams.

Your eyes may brim with tears,
Survivor spotted, maybe one safe yet,
You view the scene and stem your fears.
Sudden crack, falling marionette.

Sioux warriors on horseback slew.
Only took what they needed,
And ensured the young buffalo grew,
The spirit world was heeded.

They revered the mighty beast,
Clothing, food, shelter, everything.
After the hunt, the tribe would feast.
Tatanka, Tatanka they would sing!

Blackfoot boy made curiosity brave,
Seen the symbols in the cave.
Scrabbling into the Lakeside Lodge,
Wary of watcher's hands to dodge.

But he can twist, turn and run,
Hearing the stamping Dance to the Sun.
Adorned with Headdress, horns and feather,
Bones and beads on braided leather.

Intensified drumbeat as they dance,
Watching, his spirit in a trance.
Although he knows it's not true,
Sees Bison circling smoky hue.

Perhaps the modern world will muse,
How grazing prevented wildfire spread.
As they review the global news,
Why don't we live with nature, not wish it dead?

Jurassic Joke

Deep as hades, black as coal,
Loch Ness an early Jurassic bowl.
Shallow 'end' 80 fathoms down,
Lives a beast who wears a crown.

Many sightings from year to year,
Keeps the tourist trade in cheer.
But, out on canoe or a boat,
You pray to keep that craft afloat.
Was that a shadow in the mist,
Or geese caught in a lover's tryst?

One hundred fathoms down, we'll get there soon,
Nessie; We know more about the moon.
A creature from our history book,
Couldn't we just take a look?
But then we'd spoil the mystery,
Nessie makes more than a distillery.

The loch is far more than that,
On the move never flat.
Surrounded demonic mountains blue,
Reflecting in the water's hue.
Gulls soaring, swooping, swirling attend,
Where does the mountain, loch, horizon end?
Why do we need a monster twee,
With beauty there for all to see?

Could it be Again?

Bubbling current smooths the stone,
Cleaves the weed, like flesh from bone.
Finds the way towards the sea,
Down the slopes and in the lea.

Grows, meandering through the dale,
A path by rock or through the shale.
Scourging beds of gravel and chalk,
Ensuring clean water babble and talk.

Glides, creases, eddies seen,
Flowing around a rock unseen.
Water will always find a way,
Although much loved, it won't stay.

A darting trout, oft unseen,
Lithe Grayling, the river Queen.
Silver roach in streamer, hide,
Wary of the pike inside.
Green and gold and rictus smile,
Menace twinned with evil guile.
A Damsel nymph escapes the bed,
A fearsome dragon flies instead.

Otter parents play with pups,
Watchful Vixen quietly sups.

Activity before angler arrives,
Wiping sleep from his eyes.

Morning stream gives off a mist,
As if a river angel kissed.
If I left this world today,
Hope that heaven is this way.
A glimpse of paradise is there,
Only seen by those who care.

Mother Love

Riding submerged kelp aswirl,
Loving the savage bump and whirl.
Pulsating colours of emotion,
Feeling the rhythm of the ocean.

Her soft invertebracy skin,
Hides the warrior within.
She is the mistress of disguise,
Only uses the skill, when wise.
Can mimic shell or something live,
If prey or predator should arrive.

Wild octopus, deep in forest kelp,
No other parent there to help.
Cherishes her young, life to give,
3 hearts, 2 for love, one to live.

The male has fled, his role complete,
Father banished by peck of her beak.
Perpetual movement, surround her brood,
The pyjama shark searching for food.
Cephalopod ink, luminosity cloud,
Fits her shape just like a shroud.

She builds a fortress from nearby shells,
She fools them, gives away no tells.

As the fateful day comes near,
She mutilates herself, oh dear.
And when her young see the day,
Their sweet mum is in decay.

A mother's love as deep as this,
To kill herself in sheer bliss?
Pulsing red, blue, silvery grey,
Now sloughed dead skin, floats away.

Two Swallows Don't Make a Summer

On late summer evenings gone,
When shadows are chased or long.
We would walk the flowered fields,
Hand in hand, the sun to yield.

Heard the beaks clicking tries,
Towards us flitting, catching flies.
They fly, skimming low for fun,
More side-steps than Barry John.

Fly; cherished summer swallow,
Swooping, deft, watch them follow.
They dive around us, blue and white,
Touching, but not quite.

Their flowing tails and short wings,
Ideal for chasing tiny things.
Sometimes catch a glimpse of red,
No prettier sight, it has been said.

Higher, the swift's harangue,
Shapely sonic boomerang.
Always on the wing, no perch to think,
Dipping the lake they sip a drink.

Darker in colour and in mood,
Screaming as they capture food.
Warn the martins, flying nearby,
'A change of life' we hear them cry.
'We do everything in the air,
No time to perch and stare.

Dreamless sleep on the run,
Little time for any fun.
Martins join the swallows below,
Time to change, we should know'.

Resting your head on my shoulder,
Aware we were a little older.
The setting of the sun more poignant,
Perhaps knowing; what they meant.

Royal Salvation

Serenely circles the boating lake,
Unruffled, stately, more laps to make.
S-shaped neck and wings half mast,
A yacht less regal may have passed.

More Grace than Kelly,
Or even the ballet.
Surely the Bolshoi in every pose,
Not sure if she's on her toes.

Above the ripple she looks so neat,
But lower, webbed frenzy feet.
She hisses, strangulated call,
Less of a honk more of a bawl.

Mimic toy ostrich at the Fair,
Bottom up and beak down there.
Grubbing in the silt for worms,
Dignity waived, but on her terms.

Children, lakeside throwing food,
Joyful Sunday summer mood.
The swans swimming, oh so free,
Protected by a Royal decree.

Taking notice a conductor's que,
A cygnet glides into view.
Nothing more beautiful, a mother's eye,
Oblivious to all, this gangly guy.

Ugly duckling? Furrowed brow,
Literary licence used somehow.
A nursery rhyme overplayed,
Children spot that charade.

Eyes to charm the coldest heart,
Coy smile also plays the part.
Down as soft as winter snow,
Velvet in the afterglow.

A Regal need for softer sleep,
Duck feather not worth a peep.
Use cygnet pillows in their stead,
Fit for a Queen to rest her head.

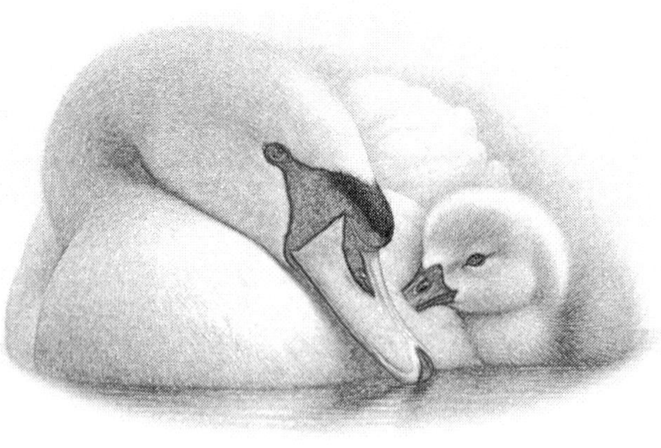

Princess of the Desert

The burning land is a red sunrise,
Reflected in a Hawk's tawney eyes.
As she soars, sees teeming life,
Eyes not so sharp, see burning strife.

Weightless feathers, lighter tones,
Massive wingspan – hollow bones.
Days without drinking only from prey,
Rodent infestation, without her say.

The Princess of the desert kills,
For her chicks, not for thrills.
A rodent moves it takes a chance,
Protecting desert eco-balance.

Jack Rabbit has dared to tread,
Seeking shade in a cacti bed.
Soundless swoop, claws extended,
Another short life has ended.

Not for her the rough-hewn hood,
No day, no night understood.
Trained by men, sporting kill,
Against her nature, creeping chill.

Falconers come in different guise,
The Peregrine set and the hawking guys.

Monocled toffs with Oxbridge lilt,
Scottish castle, they own no kilt.
Train Peregrine with the lure,
Find the Hawking men obscure.

Their turn of phrase meant to mock,
Hawkers are men from different stock.
Trained their hawks from whence they came,
Made them kill, just the same.

These men breed birds as prey,
Fly their pet Hawks to slay.
Falconers, rough hands, shouldered gun,
Keeping a slave to have some fun.

Raptor slave trade, early dawn,
Young and old and some un-born.
They duck and dive the law that's there,
Especially at a grand a pair.

'Want an eagle, a ton I think',
Touch of the nose, a nod and a wink.
They smelt of baccy and Morgans rum,
Spit in their hands, the deal was done.

Bonded slave or hawk on glove,
Neither shown an ounce of love.
Put to work, for who's good?
Even the field-hand wore no hood.

Once more she soars the heavens high,
Only in her fleeting mind's eye.
Princess regal of Pharaoh Horus,
Joins once more the wilderness chorus.

Seeing another Hawk swoop low,
Daring her to meet the foe.
Fly: Fly wild and free,
Let's hunt together, why not three?

Sonoran red meets the blue,
The nighttime desert a different hue.
Cooler now, time to rest,
Protect the chicks within the nest.

A Glimpse of Paradise

Wading, water fast and crystal,
Steeling himself, statue still.
Meandering sweep, babbling mile,
Sceptred water on sacred isle.

Moorhen, Coot lost in reeds,
Breakfast in the streamer weeds.
Little chicks glide past on tow,
Except for a straggler, all in a row.

Angler searching for the hatch,
Ensuring his fake fly will match.
Continues upstream, watching, scanning,
His casts are short, part of planning.

Hat pulled tight, as it must,
Guarding against mischievous gust.
Matching fly, a consummate skill,
Perhaps it's in his hatband still.

Line paints pictures in the sky,
Less of a swish, more of a sigh.
The angler turns his head to see,
The flowing loop in reverie.

Backward, forward just like a clock,
Perfect rhythm, tick, tock, tick, tock.
So tranquil, he stills his walk,
His quiet helps the river talk.

The sun catches the line shimmering,
Water droplets a halo glimmering.
Against soft focus, green and gold,
Monet may have been so bold.

Lightning translucent blue and red,
Kingfisher flashes past his head.
Watches in awe, caught in wonder,
Holds his breath, the bird dives under.

Concentration lost for a second,
Forced to make a skilful mend.
Dry mayfly moves nature slow,
Unnoticed, it seems, by those below.

A sudden nudge, a surface stutter,
Heart skips a beat, starts a flutter.
Calming, he stills his breathing,
All is quiet, adrenaline soothing.

Every Sunday this is his church,
Stream flows through willow and birch.
With spirit healed, in this space,
He knew no man could build this place.

A River's Lament

Perfect to the naked eye,
Fractures hidden by brooding sky.
Guitar's acidic chords will sing,
Played stridently with a broken string.

Strong, forged from centuries past,
Lament this flow may be the last.
Once was clear, full of life,
Dying now in oozing strife.

The fish have long since gone,
The poison passed on and on.
Streamer weed once so green,
Now colour of a decaying spleen.

Above the film the dragons fly,
Far below their nymphs will die.
Amphibious creatures used to spawn,
Acrid sludge, young never born.

Coots, plovers, moorhens passed,
Couldn't make a nest to last,
Damsel, beetle, newt and snail,
Died long before the depths went stale.

A tall sentry, lonely stance,
Hopes once more the fish will dance.
Wings held tight, burglars mask,
Waits all day, a thankless task.

Mankind may have meant to care,
When swimming deaths caused a scare.
Too little, too late, not so funny,
Neither drink nor wash in shareholder's money.

Hooded Wanderer

Grey barred silver, yellow eyes,
Coiled spring tense as it flies.
Wings, chilling chevron taut,
Glinting dawn in iris caught.

Unerring gaze, in wind and rain,
Maleficent eyes, skewered pain.
Ice cold windows of the soul,
Her tenacity will take its toll.

Nest in highest rocky place,
Squabbling Eyasses kept safe.
A family, one mate for life,
Hunt and love, a paradise.

Kidnapped from this idyllic way,
In chains and hood, fateful day.
Bought and sold, evil trade,
Blood lust sated; fortunes made.

Arab prince on treasured steed,
Rapacious falcon fulfils his need.
Hooded, feted, in repose,
A careless move, lose a nose.

Prey is spotted in lightening sky,
Peregrine thrown, guttural cry.
Light is jealous of her speed,
Falcon stoops unflinching heed.

Above the target, from the sun,
Drops into a frightening run.
Shocking speed, a missile aim,
Murderous impact, effect the same.

Another time, another land,
Northern estate, chained to hand.
Barons in tweeds, excited talking,
A more grounded breed, quietly stalking.

These men paid a king's ransom,
For a bird considered handsome.
Killer bird - psychotic thrill,
Permit acquired, licence to chill.

Same hood, tresses and captive heart,
Chilling calm, the hunt to start.
The hood removed, the grey tear rings,
An eye much darker than fear it brings.

It flies, it swoops, murders pheasant,
The call, the cackle not so pleasant.
No quarter, leeway or mercy shown,
The fastest killer ever flown.

Lost City – Lost Soul

The shadows shifting left and right,
In the glistening fading light.
Sounds vibrate, some heads twisted,
Nerves on edge, night sight misted.

Cacophonous jungle noise about,
Dampens the guide's quiet shout.
'Keep to the track' he implored,
Nothing else could be explored.

The once great City had been lost,
Far flung seaways had been crossed.
Now no place for man or child,
How quickly the wild, re-wilds.

She saw a moving shadow smoulder,
Symmetry moving at her shoulder.
Shaft of light; fleeting reveal,
Jaguar male, all stealth and steel.

Languid patterned markings bore,
Muscles moved like molten ore.
Loves to swim behind his mask,
Even the caiman cannot bask.

Rosette markings with beauty spot,
Invisible unless they're not.

No blade disturbed, so soft the tread,
Fear replaced with morbid dread.

The shadow melts into the gloom,
Other prey to stalk and groom.
Breathe again, resume the gait,
She'll be back, he'll just wait.

Master of His Craft

Sleek waterproof pelt, silver sheen,
Streams of bubbles where he'd been.
The lake's aquatic angel dives,
Making worlds for other lives.

Busy dams and marshes too,
Birds and frogs thrive anew.
Woodland master teaching man,
Foresters make a better plan.

Powering paddle tail too much,
Beats Phelps to the touch.
Gnaws willow, oak and ash,
Busy on his winter stash.

Pups safe from Fox's eye,
Lodge is built, two men high.
Master builder, bark and mud,
Study him, prevent the flood.

Hunted for their pelt and scent,
Killed them off without dissent.
Almost too late senses reached,
Hunting barricades were breached.

Increasing beaver numbers seen,
As fresh water begins to clean.

Nature destroyed by mankind's waste,
Conservation heroes braced.

Urban flooding must surely come,
Our folly, idiotic martyrdom.
'Paved paradise,' said Joni M,
Developers say don't point to them.

My Darling Trish

My eyes lit on my lovely Trish,
Someone more beautiful I could not wish.
As usual a harem of men,
Unchanged from now till then.

Fair of face, shaped for Vogue,
A look in her eye, smile of a rogue.
What an icon she was back then,
Friends to women, loved by men.

We lived and loved, I saw anew,
Her life took on a different view.
Kindness, compassion and a helping hand,
To all in need, she would stand.

The light of her life was her dear Dad,
Times are good and sometimes bad.
She still hears his voice so clear,
Usually in the garden, dear.

Just behind but not very far,
Are her boys 'love you Grandma'.
They look at her with adoring eyes,
Reflected back no big surprise.

Back in the day her school report,
No wife she'll make, cruel retort.
A Fabulous wife for all to see,
When I'm gone it'll be number 3!

The Nocturnal Gardener

Loud rattling spikey urging,
Tiggy-Winkle awakes emerging.
Ten gardens for her to tend,
Fences, neighbours must never mend.

Urban gardener's friend indeed,
Eats the slugs not the seed.
Newly mown grass, scents evening mood,
Gentle stroll to feed her brood.

Trail Camera showing softer sight,
White eyes seen in laser light.
Ignoring milk, must resist,
But feline food can't be missed.

Creep crawl on the banquet table,
Fallen fruit, treasure fable.
Rotted seat: grubs asleep,
Snuffling worms from compost heap.

Gardens seemingly searched anew,
Chomping delicacy in evening dew.
Squidgy slug, scoffed in delight,
Dangerously forgets dawning light.

Heading home, no time to dally,
Short-cut taken through the alley.
One last road, she's hypnotised,
Will she see the next sunrise?

Leaf-house nest, Mum is late,
Was that her spines on the gate?
Her warm milk, the hoglets wean,
Then mum snuggles close in between.

Ol' Blue eyes

Sleekly liquid feline pace,
Muscles stealing red hind's space.
Flows stealthy unseen by prey,
Until they know it's their last day.

Tawny coat, piratical beard,
Blue eyes but always feared.
Moving sinewy steel to bite,
Powerful jaws lock on tight.

Coyote howls to the lonely moon,
Whisker flicker protects her boon.
White muzzle now painted red,
Calls lowly for his mate to tread.

With man encroaching, can't roam far,
Dodging bullets and their car.
Chase a jogger, a hiker too,
No deer left they'll have to do.

Territory diminished, wolf pack roam,
Grizzly robs them of their home.
Cougar, Puma, Mountain Lion,
Many-named cat continues dying.

Losing sheep peddled excuse,
Killer cat has no use.
Illegal hunting to placate,
Head on a wall that's her fate.

Counting down, Rockies king,
Stand by, don't do a thing.
Wake up, it's later than you think,
Blue-eyed cat becoming extinct.

Big Red

We were travelling the old outback – my Abbo mate and me
dry miles went by at a searing rate – a blistering bowl of dust
first nation people went walk-about – dreamtime meant to be
living alongside the spirit world – communing as they must.

It was once the promised land – now the new country
everything kills in this strange world – humans out of place
where the natural world exists – together in harmony
exploring minds changed the map – a culture to displace.

We photographed the kangaroo – a leaping V.I.P.
he kicked off on those big red legs – in dusty reverie.

The Quiet

Silence: awakening woodland listens,
Purpling forest carpet glistens.
Stilled the popping of the broom,
Spasmodic calls break the gloom.

Head on swivel, Tubular Bells,
Wide-eyed Owl awaits the tells.
Rodents scurrying unaware,
Feathers fail to vibrate the air.

Softly swoop talons extend,
Vole or mouse eviscerating end.
Chilling elegant killing display,
Tawney swoops the rodent prey.

Quiet; cheating whisper tricks,
Gentle flight home to the chicks.
Soulmate back, love abounds,
Touching beaks, throaty sounds.

Not in a hollow, but oaken box,
Nesting place, to hide from fox.
Feathered fingers never built,
A box to counter human's guilt.

Most endangered bird of prey,
Foresters, gardeners saved the day.
Owl family now watched with care,
Again, his flight will quiet the air.

THE CHESS PIECE LEGACY

Mighty Mammoth once paced the trail,
Elephant troop marching trunk to tail.
Old Queen mum tracing tracks,
Greater dynasty from eons back.

African bull a frightening sight,
Angry elephant joined to fight.
Huge ears fanned, tusks pointing front,
Raised periscope trunk will confront.

Asian cousin safe from spears,
Longer trunk and smaller ears.
Hindu Lord, still works the field,
Elephants loved but made to yield.

Different ears, laterally lain,
Cools the body and the brain.
Trunks fingers, pick highest fruit,
Smell the big cat in pursuit.

Endangered species hope intact,
Dichotomy of a circus act.
Precious teeth set their fate,
Ivory Knights in poacher's crate.

Again, and again the conflict bites,
Man, and animal contest the rights.
Farmers with their crops to grow,
Plant them where the herds would go.

Mysterious beast from centuries past,
Caring families and love to last.
Visit the moon but will never know,
Where elephants die when not on show.

Schools Out

Sonar clicks beneath the swell,
Tells the pod that all is well.
Diving, leaping having fun,
Heading for the mackerel run.

Bluenose chatting ten to dozen,
Teasing fun with porpoise cousin.
Flashing innocent child-like smile,
Hiding all that innate guile.

Blue, silver smoothing glisten,
Loves to speak, likes to listen.
On the surface a wary eye,
Orca silhouette darkens sky.

Black and white killer, see the fin,
They are related, different kin.
Passing interest, calves not meals,
Orca chasing streamlined seals.

Broken quiet heard far away,
Mum senses others at play.
She can feel the pod's new mood,
As they near the source of food.

Caution used, just a token,
Evening, sleeping one eye open.
Watch the school and the shark,
Especially in the quiet and dark.

Another mile, should not fret,
Ceasing cry, 'Are we there yet?'
Huge joint family picnic day,
Herding circling shoals of prey.

Oily sea, hunting aftermath,
In a mackerel bubble bath.
Farewells to other schools,
Kids 'tail-walking', playing fools.

Carefree days, no black thought,
No fishing line or netting caught.
Shun the prey not swimming true,
Or be entree on Asian menu.

Clever Dolphin in coral rock,
Sponge on nose, safe from shock.
Brain size equals humans too,
Only wish we could talk to you.

A Marriage Made in Heaven

Pawnee brave leads a mustang west,
Paid with a smoked-softened buckskin vest.
Daydream hunting, Buffalo of course,
Firing arrows astride his horse.

Arabian Prince, eyes on fire,
Thoroughbred stallion, heart's desire.
His trainer nods from the back,
Soon be winning on the track.

Queen resplendent red and gold,
Chestnut mount, just as bold.
Trots along in perfect time,
Horsewoman supreme, in her prime.

Irish trainer, scans and traces,
Hunter going through her paces.
Shorter to shoulder than the crowd,
But heart of lion, makes him proud.

Suffolk punch strains on reign,
Pulling plough through wind and rain.
Without old Scottie, no planting done,
Harvest failure to overcome.

Into the valley death all around,
Steed racing covering ground.
No backward step, rode with pride,
Into hell with friend astride.

Olympian god's message sent,
Winged Pegasus no rider meant.
Conquering giants and our fears,
Painted with his daughter's tears.

If there was common sense of course,
The Latin for noble would be horse.
Head held high, a flick of mane,
Touch of arrogance, slightly vain.

Workhorse, racer, pageant queen,
Many guises can be seen.
Equestrian pair, or child's new pony,
Humankind and horse in harmony.

How Much is that Doggie in the Window

Canine pet who are you?
Pet shop purchase or dog rescue.
Caution using on-line ease,
Puppy farms, breed disease.

Hang-dog eyes, branded ‘cute’,
Handbag dogs, child substitute.
Film star symbol plays the part,
Humble mongrel gives her heart.

German shepherd faith beguiles,
Written in a grandsons’ smiles.
Sensing second guessing mood,
Faithful, fearless not just for food.

Labrador giving rides for favours,
Pulled ears and tail never wavers.
Sits quiet busy road display,
Blind Mistress walking on his say.

Collie protects the herds at night,
Fox or stray, he’ll stay and fight.
Morning comes nip their heels,
Guides them as the shepherd kneels.

Next dog disaster should take care,
Don’t blame the dog, beware.
Past or present love neglect,
A bad owner was the architect.

Before we drive, we pass a test,
For living animal, it must be best.
If dog ownership is truly sought,
Train owners before the pet is bought.

Baby, You Were Born to Run

Loping tawny buff and black,
Savannah grasses at her back.
Sudden movement, on all fours,
Ears laid back, quivering jaws.

Her head is low, shoulders high,
Long grass hides her tensing lie.
Stalks her prey, in day-time light,
Wary not to spook their fright.

Spindly legs pumped-up chest,
A lethal killer, a heartless jest?
Sprightly gazelle best take heed,
Can't outrun the Cheetah's speed.

Black tear-stained creamy mask,
Jaws will meet the killing task.
Cute ears, button nose, black spots,
Longer tail for sudden stops.

Antelope winged as in flight,
Followed by a beam of light.
Agile dancing speed to burn,
Cheetah matching twist and turn.

Prey caught, suffocate, subdue,
Dragged from jackal's thieving view.
Survival sustained; cubs will eat,
Mother chirrups for a treat.

Wandering mum with cubs in tow,
Ensures her tread is soft and slow.
Hyenas, lions kept at bay,
Only hunting in the day.

Dwindling stolen habitat it seems,
Ethereal Cheetah only in dreams.
Eroded genes lost the code,
Nightmarish extinction episode.

When they're gone, lost from view,
Most beautiful predator, now so few.
AI images shape Grandson's brain,
Show noble queen in her domain.

A Child's Comfort

Tear-stained faces, hidden bruise,
No tea tonight, did they light the fuse?
What's happened to the little dears,
Bravely holding back, their tears.

Attending school, late - again,
It's not the school that wields the cane.
Soon left behind, can't write or draw,
No bedtime reading, but 'Clean the floor!'

Heartless mother in her ivory tower,
Unwashed, the starving children cower.
Lying fearful on the filthy floor,
As drunken 'Daddy' slams the door.

How strange in the 'wild' or nest,
'Civilised' parenthood at its best.
Mothers willingly give their lives,
Teach, ensuring young survives.

Fearsome Grizzly standing tall,
Strikes alarm to one and all.
But that mum has cubs to tend,
Any danger she will defend.

Grizzly mum loving, kind,
Cubs will scratch but never mind,
She only wants to tend and teach,
Human depths she'll never reach.

Brown and Black bear, know the pain,
Poachers take their cubs again.
Protecting young from slavery,
Beheaded hung, no clemency.

Ripped from mother, caged for life,
Illegal zoo, pace in strife.
Lonely cubs die in squalor,
Weeping child knows cradle horror.

When abused children need someone,
Hope is lost, who will come.
Finding hugs and love so true,
From bears like Rupert, Ted, and Pooh.

Stolen Ponies

Sunrise spills across prairie gold,
Hawk on high foreseeing fate.
Eight mounted shadows still, unfold,
Cree scout low, hunter trait.

Scalp painted black and red,
Crinkling eyes scan for clues.
Eagle feathers adorn his head,
Glinting sunlight changing hues.

Tracking braves, of a different paint,
Snorting pony paws the ground.
Eyes sharp, spot spoor so faint,
Tribe's mustangs must be found.

Smells the woodsmoke in the morning air,
By nightfall he'll have their hair.

Woodpecker Soul?

Flocking birds - will feeder cope?
Bill and Maggie wait in hope.
Fingers crossed use special seed,
Woodpecker feigns to feed.

Days, months, years go by,
Hoping that their bird will fly.
Bird feeding a thankless deed,
If your favourite will not feed.

Hands clasped, eyes will mist,
If one should pass a lover's tryst.
Soulmate returns in the guise,
As Spotted Woodpecker before their eyes.

That fateful day did arrive,
One left alone to grieve and cry.
Sitting alone at the window seat,
Wishing for an impossible feat.

Sudden blur red, black and white,
Woodpecker lands to Bill's delight.
Science, logic can't hear that call,
Unquenchable love indeed conquers all.

SOUNDS LIKE TOM

If ever a bird has his say,
Surely it must be African Grey.
Kept on board to a sailor's delight,
Mac talked a lot, swore a mite.

Tom's ship ended an eight-year tour,
Took Mac home, no wish to soar.
Walked around the leafy shade,
Marched aloof as if on parade.

Two old aunties came for tea,
Need to silence Mac's repartee.
Cage was covered just in case,
Can't risk language quite so base.

Bone China cups moved, chink, clink,
Biscuits snapped, brew the drink.
Past re-lived, tea poured apace,
The slightest breeze ruffled lace.
A chink of light was all Mac needed,
Blasphemous squawks now heeded.

Looks of horror from Mum and Dad,
Mac's swearing was twice as bad.
The aunties remarked with aplomb,
'Why, that parrot sounds just like Tom'.

WILL NATURE FORGIVE US?

Elephant in the room it seems,
Debate forbidden, use other themes.
Eight billion people, growing fast,
Other species, forgotten past.

Wreck the planet, the air we breathe,
The seas, the rivers, no reprieve.
Recycle, re-use, grow your own,
Never ceasing to atone.

Breeding increased herds of cattle,
Are we fighting a losing battle?
Three rivers spew plastic, so readily,
What clean ocean will our children see?

Use rivers as sewers, only pay a fine,
Poison the fish, are we next in line?
Politicians evade the truth, I suspect,
Too many people, why object?
We get the allergies, e coli and cancers,
Do they care, they have no answers.

In the race who loses; us or nature,
Betrayed and murdered by profiteers.
Humans didn't craft paradise so pure,
Built hell carved in bloody tears.

We Need a Bigger Boat

Moody skies paint the swell below,
Helping green plant jungles grow.
Blue CO^2 stored in carbon forests,
Plant eating shoals that never rest.

Without a controller of the spread,
The multitude cause sheer havoc instead.
Shark the saviour, since time began,
Five extinctions, the sixth is man.

Not warm and cuddly, with panda eyes,
Stories painted to despise.
Menace with a rictus grin,
Cold hearted killer with a fin.

Fin cleaving waves apart,
Melts below and terror starts.
Much maligned by salty tales,
That evil villain, the sailor pales.

Jaws first two notes, realise the plight,
Great White attacks with speed of light.
Turbulent ocean seems to gloat,
It's clear they need a bigger boat.

Shark though has much more to fear,
Numbers down year on year.
Overfished and trapped in lines,
Least loved warrior of our times.

Heaven Must Wait

The sea is angry

angry at the Gods
for barring Poseidon his rightful place
no more treacherous sandal trod
neither Trident nor storm erase.

The sea is angry

angry at the sky
for jealously guarding heaven's gate
gulls wheel, stoop and cry
even they are nearer fate.

The sea is angry

angry with the world
unleashed typhoon and gale to teach
lashed the mountains, fury unfurled
no respite found on any beach.

The sea is angry

angry at man
wilfully poisoning the tide and swell
healthy oceanic colours ran
mercy me, hells' tolling bell.

The sea is calm

calmer still is Poseidon
man has gone, quieter blows the gale
wistfully scanning far horizon
disappointed no distant swirl of sail.

The Wedding

Dawn cirrus, pinking awakening sky,
Soft cool morning breeze a sigh.
River meandering stretches away,
White-bottomed doe blinks the day.

High sharp cheek bones, green-grey eyes,
Viewed handsome, by some other tribes.
Spirit stirred hears eagle speak,
'Good day for wedding, the one you seek'.

Cherokee Chief keeps feelings at bay,
Daughter will wake to her wedding day.
Views tribes' teepees from higher ground,
Watching preparation of ritual mound.

Buffalo teepees in hierarchy stood,
Ceremonial fires three stacks of wood.
Two fires alight, for bride and groom,
Join Great Spirit's rising plume.

Sees below, groom's wedding gift,
Snorting wild-eyed pony shift.
Daughter's blue handprint bedeck,
A mustang's golden arching neck.

Dressing regal for meeting ground,
His humming heart makes no sound.
Bison bone pins in braided hair,
Beads of turquoise teeth of bear.

Emerges into the throng of elders,
Blue blanket adorns daughter's shoulders.
Eyes held proud, takes her stand,
Gold eagle feathers in her hand.

Wives place sacred vase then bow,
White blankets for the final vow.
All this is done with love and care,
Sweet sage smoke fills the air.

Looks to distant higher ground,
Hears rising raucous sound.
Neighbours escort one of their sons,
Singing, whooping, thumping drums.

Blue blanketed groom set to ground,
Clasping feather; stands, no sound.
Bride shares the vase a look so fond,
Drinking together secures the bond.

Chief, so proud, but softly cries,
Links their hands, hears their sighs.
Sees in the eyes of his new son,
Portent, of stormier times to come.

Fishers of Men

Babbling crystal, wetland dark,
Silted lake, pond in the park.
Meandering river, stream in strife,
Foaming weir, homes to life.

Bars of silver, roach fin red,
Boy catches, he's hooked instead.
Captivated for lifetime sure,
Loves the chase, to the core.

Carp, translucent scales by rank,
Viewing monsters from the bank.
Swirl on the top, splash in the sun,
Must be a heifer jumped in for fun.

Bearded barbel torpedo slim,
How many miles do they swim?
Grubbing silt for mollusc and worm,
Watchful eye for Heron and Tern.

Raising her net with wondrous whoop,
Caught a 'stripey' first flourishing scoop.
Olive with black bars, dorsal fin spike,
A beautiful perch not a scary old pike.

Chalk stream clear or Loch in thunder,
All species swimming adds to wonder.
Whether sturgeon top of the pile,
Or minnows just here for a while.
Fresher waters poisoned anew,
We are left with a dwindling few.
Lost now, the wonder in a child's eye,
To watch from the bank as the fish swim by.

PRIDE

Proud head lifted to Savanna dawn,
The King stretches a mighty yawn.
Looks lovingly at his lounging pride,
Eyes chance upon his newest bride.

Her hunter's movement, svelte and grace,
Her quieter tread, as soft as lace,
Nuzzles cubs who mewl and play,
Gentle paw ensures their stay.

Sleep feigned roosting in a tree,
Lion King protects his family.
Wary of cowering Hyena band,
Born cowards refuse to make a stand.

The sun recedes a shimmering ball,
Maned male growls hunting call.
His Highness and the cubs kept back,
Lionesses start to scent and track.

The girls bring gazelle to ground,
The cubs and pride gather round.
Soon they'll be wearing ruby masks,
Another feed and cleaning tasks.

The King rolls over on his side,
Work now done by rest of pride.
What a life, if you don't tire,
His only chore, cubs to sire.

Can't Change His Spots

Rippling, muscular, ethereal-grey,
Shunning hunt in searing day.
Eyesight keen, whetted blade,
Blackest night sees no shade.

Head slunk low, hovering tail,
Hunting leopard rarely fail.
Grating City sounds to hear,
Nothing escapes the velvet ear.

Perfume, straying, fetid stink,
Ignored; flowing, stalking slink.
A scent, stench can never quell,
Excited by that porcine smell.

Spectre appears from the night,
Piglets squealing in anxious fright.
Hysterical running, mustn't dally,
Their die is cast, the blindest alley.

Feline killer leaps away,
Carries concrete-jungle prey.
Rag dolly without a dress,
Mother boar one piglet less.

Jungle canopy, sepulchral spires,
High rise slum, ghetto pyres.
Adapting leopard calls the shots,
After all, he can't change his spots.

MERLINA'S PERCH

Ghostly Tower in rising mist,
Watcher's quiet unsettling calm.
Twinkling capital river kissed,
Raven satin feathers balm.

Wrinkling orange peel claw,
Wilderness reflecting blackened eye.
Priestess, not above the law,
Sorceress profile, silken sky.

Protecting keys to nation's heart,
If they should fly, the King will fall.
Tearing, tearing, worlds apart,
We'd never hear the Raven's call.

Rocky, don't you play the fool,
Erin, stoic won't show the pain.
Harris wants to go to school,
Gripp plays Dicken's pet again.

Ragged band surveyed on high,
Another Jubilee is crying.
Merlina issues startled cry,
Time to go, ol' Blighty's dying.

Red-Breasted Warrior

Whistling, melodic strident note,
Temper fiery as its feathered coat.
Spikey, truculent, lion-heart mum,
Alarms the cat who would kill her son.

Perched on handle of garden fork,
Discarded before a morning walk.
Soil, freshly tilled, compost black,
Anxious worms readying for attack.

Robin's banquet, only brave will feed,
Squidgy worms, keep your seed.
Warbling thrush, fluttering finch,
Even make a blackbird flinch.

Oh, what joy in winter's hours,
Robin's tumultuous melody towers.
As swelling song begins to race,
Grandson turns his smiling face.

Forever yours this badge of courage,
A breast of fire for your homage.
Clear to see the Saviour's blood,
Splashed before the cross you stood.

Thank you once again for supporting

The RUR River Charity

Acknowledgements

My main thank you is to my long-suffering wife, chief listener, critic and rock. Her infectious positivity has kept me going. There is a little love poem in the middle of the collection, so I will find out if she really reads this book!

My thanks also to all at Olney writing group, especially Lizzie and Mike for the supportive listening as I would enthusiastically launch into one of my renditions, unconsciously interrupting their coffee morning. Also, Dan for his superb understanding of the pictorial technology and to Sue for her support and guiding hand on the tiller.

Thanks must go to my main writing mentor TC, who steadfastly read, grammar checked and critiqued my work. Lastly, but certainly not least, my gratitude goes to Deb for her creative use of technology in the illustrations, her publishing knowledge, and for driving the book to print.

About the Author

James spent the last 15 years of his working life with two brilliant partners, running their own training and coaching company called T3 web. His training style was based on 20 years of selling and marketing for BT and IBM, into large and small corporate companies.

James was the first salesman in his company to graduate from Leeds University with separate diplomas in sales and marketing. His mainly technical education left little room for his main loves, the natural world, indigenous cultures and reading. However, he recently joined the Olney writing group and found inspiration in the world of poetry.

The motivation drove him, in a very short time, to follow his heart. He has used poetry as a medium to highlight the plight of some of nature's most valuable gifts.

Printed in Great Britain
by Amazon

df2d1391-d3f6-4812-ae58-981a7eb37f43R01